Kabir Ke 50 Dohe

Kabir Ke 50 Dohe

50 Lessons on Entrepreneurship

(Connecting Ancient Indian Wisdom with Entrepreneurship)

(With Couplets in Hindi Explained in English and Connecting with Entrepreneurship)

Prof (Dr) Sanjeev Chaturvedi

GenNext Publication

Published by

GenNext Publication
5, Ansari Road
Daryaganj, New Delhi-110002
Phone: 011-47034999, 9811692060
E-mail: gennextpublication@hotmail.com

Distribution Network
gyanbooks.com
India, USA, Canada, UK, Australia, France

ISBN: 978-93-5663-788-7 (PB)

First Published, 2024

Printed at: Gyan Press, Delhi.

This book is dedicated to
my mother Late Shrimati
SHEELA CHATURVEDI
(Ammaji)

Acknowledgement

This book is a small effort to connect Ancient Indian Wisdom with Modern Form of Entrepreneurship. I must thank first to Geeta Press, Gorakhpur, India for providing one of the best books on various subjects since 1923. It has been a great help in writing this book with their diverse publications on Kabir.

Secondly, I would like to thank all my teachers/ professors/friends and family members who supported me in writing my previous 5 books and got good response from readers. Their positive response encouraged me to write this Third book on Entrepreneurship and connecting it with Ancient Indian Wisdom. I would also like to thank my critics who gave me the fire in belly, to prove them wrong, at all stages. This book could not be completed without the support and love of my wife Richa and my two beautiful children Vartika and Vedant.

I am highly obliged to Garg Publishers, New Delhi who have been constantly supporting me in my publications for a long time. My special thanks to their Editor Mr. Garg and his team for supporting me in giving final touches and shape to this book.

Finally, I now present this book to all my readers with great humility and modesty, for allowing me to write a book connecting Kabir and Entrepreneurship. I am confident that my mistakes will be ignored and encouragement will be given for making this humble attempt.

For suggestions, comments, criticism etc.
write to me on my personal email id:
sanjeev.chaturvedi2015@gmail.com

Who was Kabir Das

Kabir Das was a 15th-century Indian mystic poet and saint. His writings influenced Hinduism's Bhakti movement, and his verses are found in Sikhism's scripture Guru Granth Sahib, the Satguru Granth Sahib of Saint Garib Das, and Kabir Sagar. Kabir was born in 1398 in city Banaras, now called Varanasi in the state of Uttar Pradesh, India. His parents name was Neeru and Nima (his caretaker parents). His parents were extremely poor and uneducated but they heartily adopted the little baby and trained him about their own business. He was brought up in Muslim family but he wrote about Principles of Life. His parents were weaver by Profession.

Kabir Das believed in the **Formless God**. His teachings were followed by people from different communities. In the 15th century, when Persian and Sanskrit were predominant North Indian languages, he chose to write in colloquial, regional language. Not just one, his poetry is a mixture of Hindi, Khari boli, Punjabi, Bhojpuri, Urdu, Persian and Marwari.

Teaching

Kabir Das **tried to coordinate the religions by giving a universal path which could be followed by all human beings**. According to him, every life has a relationship with two spiritual principles (Jivatma and Paramatma). His view about the moksha is that it is the process of uniting these two divine principles.

The major ideas expressed by Kabir include: **Rejection of major religious traditions. Criticism of all forms of external worship of both Brahmanical Hinduism and Islam. Criticism of priestly classes and the caste system.**

He believed in the oneness of God and opposed the idea of worshipping the idols. Kabir emphasised the need to persistently purify the soul to be close to God rather than to indulge in various rituals.

It is considered that he got all his spiritual training from his Guru named, Ramananda, in his early childhood. One day, he became a well-known disciple of guru Ramananda. Kabir Das house has been accommodated for students and scholars for living and studying his great works.

It is believed that he received his spiritual lessons from Guru Ramananda of Sant Kabir. Initially, Ramananda did not agree to consider Kabir Das his disciple. Once upon a time, Saint Kabir Das was lying on the steps of a pond and was reciting the mantra of Rama-Rama, Ramananda was going to bathe in the morning and Kabir came under his feet. Ramanand felt guilty for that activity and Kabir Das ji urged him to accept him as his student. It is believed that Kabir family still lives in Kabir Chaura, Varanasi.

Siddhapeeth Kabirchaura Math Mulgadi and his Tradition

Kabirchaura Math Mulgadi is the home, historical work place and meditation place of the Saint-Shiromani Kabir Das. He was the only saint of his type, known as the "Sab Santan Sartaj". It is considered as the history of humanity is worthless without Kabirchaura Math Mulgadi just like all the saints are valueless without Saint Kabir. Kabirchaura Math Mulgadi has its own affluent traditions and effective history. It is the home of Kabir as well as the courageous Vidyapeeth for all the saints. The Indian saints of the Madhyakalin India got their spiritual education from this place. It has been proved in the history of human tradition that it is not necessary to go to the Himalayas for deep meditation, but it can be done by living in the society. Kabir Das himself was the ideal indication of this. He is the real indication of the Bhakti, living together with the normal human being life. He showed the way of free Bhakti to the people instead of worshipping stone.

1

बड़ा हुआ तो क्या हुआ जैसे पेड़ खजूर।
पंथी को छाया नहीं फल लागे अति दूर।।

Meaning

It is of no use being very big or rich if you don't do any good to others. For example, a palm tree is so tall; however, it is of no use to a traveler because it provides no shade, and the fruit is also at the top. Thus, none can eat it easily.

Lesson for Entrepreneurs

Kabir here tries to say that if you are a successful entrepreneur and have made lots of profits in your business. But it will be worthless if you have not shared it with the people, who made you successful and helped you to reach that success. The success and profits will be worthless if it is not used for society's benefit as a whole. Hence, we should always be sharing our profits and money with the employees, stake holders and society at large. Then actually we will be called successful Entrepreneurs.

2

कबीरा खड़ा बाजार में, सबकी मांगे खैर।
ना काहू से दोस्ती, ना काहू से बैर।।

Meaning

One should always think well of everyone. There is no need to be over-friendly with anyone, nor should you be hostile to anyone.

Lesson for Entrepreneurs

Kabir here like to give us a message that in business there is no friend and no enemy. Business has to be done without bringing emotional quotient in the process. Once enemy, can be friends and once friends, can be enemy/competitor in business. Hence, we should always take our business above everything without being overfriendly or over enmity.

3

कहे कबीर कैसे निबाहे, केर बेर को संग।
वह झूमत रस आपनी, उसके फाटत अंग।।

Meaning

People who are different cannot live together. If bananas and ber (jujube) trees are planted near each other, the ber tree will swing in the air, whereas banana tree leaves will get torn by its thorns.

Lesson for Entrepreneurs

The lesson we get from Kabir in this couplet is that we should have a team which is of like minded people, so that all should work in One Direction and for One Goal. If we have very different thinking people in our firm/company then we can be losing our direction and goals. There will be always difference and conflicts in working. Lots of time will be lost and wasted in resolving them and wasting our energy and efforts. Hence, we should always select our employees very carefully.

4

तिनका कबहूँ न निदिंये, जो पावन तर होए।
कभू उडी अखियाँ परे तो पीर घनेरी होए।।

Meaning

You should not oppress the weak as you should not trample a speck. When that weak person counterattacks, it will be very painful. Just like a speck of dust in the eye can cause a lot of discomfort.

Lesson for Entrepreneurs

Kabir here wants to give this message that we should always take good care of people including our juniormost employees. It is not prudent to focus only on big people or customer and neglect the smaller ones. For a successful Entrepreneur everyone is equal and everyone deserves equal importance and attention. Only then you will be successful entrepreneur.

5

साँई इतना दीजिए जामें कुटुंब समाय।
मैं भी भूखा ना रहूँ साधु न भूखा जाय।।

Meaning

Kabir requests the almighty to give him only as much as required to feed his family and if any guest comes, then he should be able to feed him too. It means you should only have what you need as there is no use in having too much.

Lesson for Entrepreneurs

It's often debated that how much money you should have to be Happy and Successful. Kabir in this couplet try to address this debate. He says that one should have enough money to meet all basic requirements of himself and his employees. All should be comfortable while working with him. All must be satisfied and happy in that company and contribute to further progress of the company and reap the benefits of such progress in long run. Hence money should neither be less or too much, but enough to satisfy all needs and requirements of the people, and make everyone happy and forward looking towards life.

6

माटी कहे कुम्हार से, तू क्या रौंदे मोय।
एक दिन ऐसा आएगा, मैं रौंदूगी तोय।।

Meaning

The soil tells the pot maker that you think you are kicking and kneading me with your feet but there will be a day when you will be below me (buried after death) and I will knead you.

Lesson for Entrepreneurs

Through this couplet of Kabir, we can derive the meaning and lesson for Entrepreneurs that they should not be arrogant with their success and richness. Ultimately nothing is permanent, Success and Money will come and go. But your behaviour towards others, your helping nature towards others and contribution to society at large will be remembered. Hence, one should be always humble in nature and behaviour, and always treat people with dignity and politeness.

7

माला फेरत जुग भया, फिरा न मन का फेर।
कर का मन का डार दे, मन का मनका फेर।।

Meaning

This is sarcasm on people who are blind followers of a religion. Kabir says you spent your life turning the beads of the rosary but could not turn your own heart. Leave the rosary and try to change the evil in your heart.

Lesson for Entrepreneurs

Kabir here says that one should not always be blind follower of anything in life. An entrepreneur should always be more rational and logical in his thinking and action. Even too much of religion following is not recommended as person can be religious in nature but should not be blind follower. An entrepreneur should always do things which not only be beneficial to others but also society at large, whichever religion they follow. This will also bring satisfaction and happiness to him which is the True Religion.

8

गुरु गोविदं दोनों खड़े, काके लागूं पाँय।
बलिहारी गुरु आपनो, गोविंद दियो मिलाय।।

Meaning

A teacher is even greater than God. Kabir quips that if the teacher and the god are both in front of him, who will he greet first? The teacher's teaching has made it possible for him to see the god.

Lesson for Entrepreneurs

Here from this couplet Entrepreneur can understand that, here Kabir wants to say that Knowledge is Supreme. Even those who teach Religion also use knowledge for propagating it to masses. It is thru knowledge only one can be superior to others. Only True Knowledge makes you successful and Only True Knowledge will be respected by the World and Humanity in long run. Hence, we should always respect True Knowledge and also respect those who give us that Knowledge i.e our Teachers and Gurus.

9

पाथर पूजै हरि मिले, तो मैं पूजू पहाड़।
घर की चाकी कोई ना पूजे, जाको पीस खाए संसार।।

Meaning

Kabir says people worship idols made from stone. If it was possible to reach the god this way, then he would worship the mountain. But, no one worships the home flour mill (chakki) which gives us the flour to eat.

Lesson for Entrepreneurs

Here Kabir was trying to say that sometime we do not give credit to those who are actually very useful to us in our business and in our life. On the other hand, we give undue importance to people who are actually are of no use and just craving for the importance given. Hence, Kabir says that we should always focus on people who are helpful to business and overall development to growth of the organisation.

10

अति का भला न बोलना, अति की भली न चूप।
अति का भला न बरसना, अति की भली न धूप।।

Meaning

Kabir Das says that too much of anything is not good. One must exercise control and be moderate in everything. Too much talking is not good, and neither is too much quietness. Just like how too much rain is not good, nor is too much sunshine.

Lesson for Entrepreneurs

Here Kabir says that as an entrepreneur, one should have a balanced life and working culture in business. Apart from Emergencies, one should create a Work- Life Balance in the organisation. This will create not only a happy and satisfied team of employees but they will also help in growth of the organisation. It is very important to see that everyone, including Entrepreneur, enjoy both his professional and personal life and lead a satisfied life.

11

तन विष की बेलरी, गुरु अमृत की खान।
शीश दियो जो गुरु मिले, तो भी सस्ता जान।।

Meaning

Kabir here says that Our Human body is full of Poisons (Doubts and Vices). But Real Teacher or Guru is like Amrit (Like Guiding force). Even if we have to give our head to find a right teacher then it will be a cheaper bargain.

Lesson for Entrepreneurs

Here we can corelate Kabir couplet who indicated that business is with full of challenges and difficulties. Hence it is very important to find out the right persons to do the right thing and take the business to next level. Sometime these people are little expensive but it is still very cheap, when we see their contribution in success of the business and profits. Hence, we should always be looking for people who are guiding force for the success of the business.

12

सब धरती काजग करू, लेखनी सब वनराज।
सात समुद्र की मसि करूँ, गुरु गुण लिखा न जाए।।

Meaning

Kabir here say that even if I make the whole earth The Paper and all trees The Pen, and even I make whole water of seven seas The Ink, even then it will be short to write the benefits I will get from a Right Guru or Right Person.

Lesson for Entrepreneurs

This couplet denotes that words will fall short if we start to explain the benefits of right people/employees in our organisation. To find a right person is the most difficult and most precious thing to do in Business. It is very important to find these people who will take business to next level of development and profits.

13

ऐसी वाणी बोलिए मन का आप खोये।
औरन को शीतल करे, आपहुं शीतल होए।।

Meaning

Kabir says that one should speak in such a manner, where it not only sound good to the persons who are listening, but it is also good listening yourself. Hence, we should be a good person to listen.

Lesson for Entrepreneurs

Through this couplet we should understand the importance of communication. It is always important to understand what to say, how to say and when to say. Good communication is the backbone of all business success. Communicating well and in right way to all stakeholders is very important. Right communication will solve most of the problems.

14

निंदक नियरे राखिये, आँगन कुटी छवाये।
बिन पानी साबुन बिना, निर्मल करे सुभाय।।

Meaning

Kabir here says that one should always keep critics near yourself, as they will always criticise you but they will always let you know what is wrong with you. They will keep you pointing your shortcomings and will help you in improving yourself.

Lesson for Entrepreneurs

Through this couplet of Kabir, we can derive that in business we should always keep our critics very close and carefully listen to them. It is important to listen to them, even if we do not like them. When we listen to them, we know that what are our shortcomings and what more we have to correct in business. We should look positively towards our criticism and take lesson out of it. We should be able to take criticism in a constructive way and improve our business, wherever required. Criticism is important for business growth.

15

बुरा जो देखन मैं चला, बुरा न मिलिया कोय।
जो मन देखा आपना, मुझ से बुरा न कोय।

Meaning

Here Kabir says that we always try to find out faults in others very easily. But when we look inside ourself we will find that we are the worst person in the world. There are so many faults within ourselves. Hence, instead of looking outwards, we should look inwards, to find faults in this world.

Lesson for Entrepreneurs

We can learn from this couplet a very important lesson for business. We should not be finding faults in our stakeholders like bankers, suppliers, employees, customers etc. But we should analyse what are the problems of our internal processes and how we can solve them. It is always easy to blame others but very difficult to understand our own business faults. We should look inside our business to solve problems, rather than looking outside and blaming others.

16

दुःख में सुमिरन सब करे, सुख में करे न कोय।
जो सुख में सुमिरन करे, तो दुःख काहे को होय।।

Meaning

Kabir here says that when we are in some trouble or sad or facing any problem we remember GOD for rescue and for solving the problem. But we never remember GOD when we are successful and happy. What if we remember the GOD in good times and if we do that, why there will be bad time. Hence, we should remember GOD in good times so that bad times does not come.

Lesson for Entrepreneurs

From this couplet of Kabir, we can understand that when the company is doing good and is successful, it forgets the people who have supported and helped the organisation. When trouble comes or company going thru the bad times, they once again start remembering the people for help. So, it will be prudent that we do not forget the people who had built the organisation and always seek their support. If this relationship continues then there will be no bad times for the company.

17

पानी केरा बुदबुदा, अस मानस की जात।
देखत ही छुप जाएगा है, ज्यों तारा परभात।।

Meaning

Kabir here wants to say that it is tendency of the human being that we have lots of Wishes during our life. When one is finished, we get another wish and we start running after that. Kabir here further says that if we get a Right Guru we will be on Right Path and we will get our Right Destination or Right Purpose of our Life.

Lesson for Entrepreneurs

From this couplet we can derive that we always as an entrepreneur or as a Businessman run for Profits and Expansion and in this way, we are never satisfied what we achieve. It is important and good to have profits in the organisation, but it should be invested back for the Society and for the people who are not privileged like others. They should be helped to stand on their own feet and to make them self-dependent. That's the True Force and Motive of Generating Profits.

18

चलती चक्की देख के, दिया कबीरा रोये।
दो पाटन के बीच में, साबुत बचा न कोए।।

Meaning

Kabir here says that when he sees grinding machine, he feels sorry as anything comes in between the two parts of Grinding Machine, nothing is left. In the same way he further adds that is life full of sadness and happiness and human being keeps on continuing their lives in between them, sometime sad and sometime happy.

Lesson for Entrepreneurs

From this couplet of Kabir, we can understand the working of an organisation. Good and bad times continue with the company and it is part of growth and further journey of any organisation. Hence, we should not be too elated when there is success and not to be disheartened when organisation is not doing well. The time will also pass like good times. Hence, we should always be focused on future rest will be taken care by the time itself.

19

मलिन आवत देख के, कलियन कहे पुकार।
फूले फूले चुन लिए, कालि हमारी बार।।

Meaning

Here Kabir says that when a gardner goes to garden, Flower Buds start discussing that today he has come to pluck full flowers and sell them in market. Similarly, tomorrow when we will become full flower, he will pluck us and sell in market.

Lesson for Entrepreneurs

From this Kabir Couplet we can derive that every organisation has a lifecycle. They start -they grow-they decline and they perish. There is no organisation in the world which can claim to be immortal. The only thing which an entrepreneur can do is to keep doing his work and continue his journey. Things will automatically take shape and further growth and further declined can only be decided by the time to come.

20

काल करे सो आज कर, आज करे सो अब।
पल में परलय होएगी, बहुरि करेगा कब।।

Meaning

Kabir in this couplet says that time is short and one does not know when the time ends. Hence, we should do today what will planned for tomorrow and do tomorrow that we planned for day after. Time is short and unknown hence we should complete everything before it's too late.

Lesson for Entrepreneurs

Kabir in this couplet points out the importance of Time Management. As an entrepreneur one should always understand the importance of Time Management. Right Thing at Right Time is the essential for any organisational success. One should plan everything and try to finish it before it's too late. Otherwise, your competitors will take advantage of your slow response and will take your market. Hence Time Management is very important for Entrepreneur to become successful.

21

ज्यों तिल माहि तेल है, ज्यों चकमक में आग।
तेरा साईं तुझ ही में है, जाग सके तो जाग।।

Meaning

Kabir here says that Til has Oil within itself and Fire has light within it, but both of them do not know. Similarly, everyone is looking for God in different worship places, not knowing that God is within you. So instead of finding God outside One should look for God within Oneself.

Lesson for Entrepreneurs

Here from this couplet of Kabir we can derive that the purpose of success of business is not just profit but it is much more than that. All success and profits of the company is not just business but it is for larger benefit for employees and people who are underprivileged. You do not have to find the true meaning of profit; it is just giving back to people from whom you have derived profit.

22

जहाँ दया तहाँ धर्म है, जहाँ लोभ वहां पाप।
जहाँ क्रोध तहाँ काल है, जहाँ क्षमा वहां आप।।

Meaning

Kabir here says that wherever there is Kindness there is Justice, wherever there is Greed there is Injustice, wherever there is Anger there is Destruction, wherever there is Forgiveness there is God. Hence, we should always be looking for these qualities in and around our life and live it to full happiness.

Lesson for Entrepreneurs

What we can derive from Kabir couplets is that all businesses see good and bad phases of business cycles. But during these times we should not succumb to Greed, Anger and Unjustified means. As these things will always take our company to losses and destruction in the long run. We should always focus on kindness, forgiveness and overall happiness of our employees and society at large. Then only your company and business will grow and prosper.

23

जो घट प्रेम न संचारे, जो घट जान सामान।
जैसे खाल लुहार की, सांस लेत बिनु प्राण।।

Meaning

Kabir here says that those people who does not have compassion and kindness for other human beings, he is just like an animal who just survive for his own self and die for own self.

Lesson for Entrepreneurs

From this couplet we can derive that those businesses, which just work for Profit of their own, there success is meaningless. They are just like animal who lives to eat to satisfy their own need of hunger. Companies who do not give back to employees and society at large, even if they are successful, their existence is meaningless in the society and corporate world.

24

जल में बसे कमोदनी, चंदा बसे आकाश।
जो है जा को भावना सो ताहि के पास।।

Meaning

Kabir here in this couplet says Lotus bloom in water pond and Moon Blooms in Sky. They are thousands of miles apart and have no connection. But when their full moon light then the image of Moon falls in water pond and both Lotus and Moon look so closely. Similarly, when person loves God, God himself comes down to Man and bless him.

Lesson for Entrepreneurs

From this Kabir couplet we should understand that there will be long path for any company to reach its destination. There will be challenges and hurdles in this path, but if the direction and dedication is there, then one day Success and Ultimate Aim of the organisation, will be achieved. Hence, one should never be afraid of challenges and hurdles of the path and work towards its Ultimate Goal.

25

जाती न पूछो साधू की, पूछ लीजिये ज्ञान।
मोल करो तलवार का, पड़ा रहने दो म्यान।।

Meaning

Kabir in this couplet say's that one should not ask the Religion and Caste of a Learned Man but look for his Knowledge and Wisdom. Because that is more important than anything else. Similarly, one should always see that how sharp is the Sword and its ability to Cut, rather than seeing the Mayan in which it is kept because that is immaterial.

Lesson for Entrepreneurs

Kabir says a very important thing here in this couplet. He says when a company is recruiting someone, they must just focus on qualification, experience and knowledge of the person. They should not be bothered from which family, which caste or which religion they come from. Because those things are immaterial. It's the qualities of individual that will help the company to grow rather than anything else.

26

ते दिन गए अकारथ ही, संगत भई न संग।
प्रेम बिना पशु जीवन, भक्ति बिना भगवंत।।

Meaning

Kabir here says that one is wasting time if he is not spending his life with good and holy people. Any person who is not doing any good work for society is also wasting his life and the purpose for which he is born. He is like an animal as he is also not following good people and not doing good deeds.

Lesson for Entrepreneurs

From this couplet of Kabir, we can derive is that a successful entrepreneur should always keep company and listen to its good advisor, who wants growth of the organisation. A good entrepreneur who are successful should always give back to its employees and society at large. It is because of them the organisation has grown and flourished. One should not forget that all these stakeholders who had made the entrepreneur successful. Without these giving back to employees/ stakeholders/ society the entire existence of the organisation and its success is meaningless and directionless.

27

तीरथ गए से एक फल, संत मिले फल चार।
सतगुरु मिले अनेक फल, कहे कबीर विचार।।

Meaning

Kabir here says that if you visit a religious place, you get One Holy Deed. But if you visit the good company of learned people you will get numberless Holy Deeds. And if you get a Good Guru or Mentor, you will be having a HOLY LIFE and your birth aim will be achieved.

Lesson for Entrepreneurs

From this Kabir Couplet we can derive the essence that a good entrepreneur when help one person it is commendable, but when he gives back to all employees of the organisation and stakeholders, he has to be applauded by us. But when an entrepreneur gives back to society then he is Great Entrepreneur. His life and his organisation become Great and Meaningful.

28

तन को जोगी सब करे, मन को विरला कोय।
सहजे सब विधि पाइए, जो मन जोगी होए।।

Meaning

Here Kabir focusses in this couplet that One always clean his body from outside. But One does not clean his body from inside. One should be having clean conscious and clean heart. Only those people are true person and human being who are pure from inside.

Lesson for Entrepreneurs

From this couplet of Kabir one can derive that it is good that organisation is successful and earning profits. But this is worthless if it does not make others happy. Hence the profit-making organisations should always share their profits and success with their employees/ stakeholders and society at large. Only then the Organisation existence and success is meaningful in the world.

29

प्रेम न बारी उपजे, प्रेम न हाट बिकाए।
राजा प्रजा जो ही रुचे, सिस दे ही ले जाए।।

Meaning

Kabir wants to say here that neither Love is grown in any agricultural field nor Love is sold in the Market. If you want Love you have to give away your Anger, Greed, Desires and Fear. Only then you will get Love after losing all these.

Lesson for Entrepreneurs

From this couplet we can derivate that if an entrepreneur want to get love and respect from his employees and society at large, he must throw away his anger, greed for money, long list of desires and fear to lose everything. If he is running behind these invaluable things, he will not earn love and respect from others. Hence one should be always working towards larger good of the society and people.

30

जिन घर साधू न पूजिये, घर की सेवा नाही।
ते घर मरघट जानिए, भुत बसे तिन माही।।

Meaning

Kabir here says that the home where there is no respect of pious people and where the truth is not worshipped, that house is filled with bad omen. That house is like a cremation ground where only dead bodies come and where only devils live.

Lesson for Entrepreneurs

From this couplet of Kabir, we can derive that those organisations which get success from illegal means and methods, those organisations are certain to collapse. These organisations are successful for short period but in long run they will doom. Hence one should not adopt shortcut methods or illegal methods to achieve success. Success journey is long and full of difficulties, but the success then is everlasting and respectable.

31

साधु ऐसा चाहिए जैसा सूप सुभाय।
सार-सार को गहि रहै थोथा देई उडाय।।

Meaning

Kabir here says that a Good Human being should act like a Filter of Food Grains. Like when we filter Food Grain through Filter, only grains remains and rest unwanted things are passed thru the Filter. Similarly, there are so many good and bad things are happening around us. A Good Human should be like this Filter, it should throw away what is bad happening around him in the world and absorb only good things from it.

Lesson for Entrepreneurs

From the above Couplet we should derive that for an entrepreneur, in the environment there must be lot of good and bad ways are open for the success of the organisation. These ways may be legal or illegal. Both options are available for the entrepreneur but a good entrepreneur should always be choosing the Right Path to achieve the growth and success of the organisation because it is everlasting and permanent.

32

पाछे दिन पाछे गए हरी से किया न हेत।
अब पछताए होत क्या, चिड़िया चुग गई खेत।।

Meaning

Kabir here says that much time has gone and person has not done anything good in life and neither he remembered the God for what he gave to him. Now the person is repenting as all-time has been wasted, but it is of no use as now the whole agriculture farm has been eaten by birds and no crop is left. Hence there is no point of repenting about the lost time, it will never come back.

Lesson for Entrepreneurs

From this couplet we can derive that there is ample opportunity for an entrepreneur to do some good deeds when he has profits and organisation is successful. However, he is so busy doing so many things which is not required and desired. At the end when the downfall of organisation come, he starts remembering that he has not done any good to his people, his employees, his stakeholders and society at large. He then starts repenting which is of no use, as the time has already gone and he cannot bring it back. Once Time is Lost it will never come back. Hence, we must do Right Things at Right Time.

33

जब मैं था तब हरी नहीं, अब हरी है मैं नाही।
सब अँधियारा मिट गया, दीपक देखा माही।।

Meaning

Kabir here says that my heart was full of darkness as I was blind with my Arrogance and Knew No God. But now I have Got God in my Heart and now there is no arrogance in my heart. It is like darkness, when there is no light there is darkness but when Light of God/Knowledge is there, then there is no darkness.

Lesson for Entrepreneurs

Similarly, an entrepreneur becomes arrogant with his success and profits and thinks he knows everything. He thinks he is the most knowledgeable person because he is successful. But when competitor comes out with better product, he realises that his knowledge is just a fraction of sea of knowledge.Then he realises that how ignorant was he in front of others wisdom and knowledge. Then true realisation comes in.

34

नहाये धोये क्या हुआ, जो मन मैल न जाए।
मीन सदा जल में रहे, धोये बास न जाए।।

Meaning

Kabir through this couplet says that it is immaterial that we clean our body from outside every day. It is more important to clean our body from inside. If our soul is not clean then there is no point in taking bath every day. It is like fish who remains in water whole life but it gives foul smell when you take it out and you have to clean it.

Lesson for Entrepreneurs

From this couplet we can derive that an entrepreneur can be successful but unless and until the means and path which are chosen by him are not clean, success is immaterial. If he has done illegal and immoral way of getting those success then it is worthless. The true success is not there, it is an Immoral Victory and Not Pure Success. Hence, entrepreneur should always take a honest and pure way to be successful.

35

प्रेम पियाला जो पिए, सिस दक्षिणा देय।
लोभी शीश न दे सके, नाम प्रेम का लेय।।

Meaning

Kabir here says that if you want God Grace then you have to leave Greed, Anger, Fear and Wishes. Only then you can get God blessings. But human being does not want to give all these unnecessary things and want to get blessing of God, which is not possible.

Lesson for Entrepreneurs

From this Kabir Couplet we can derive that if an entrepreneur wants to be successful, he must lose the anger, greed, desires etc which are never ending and never fulfilled. He must focus on the welfare of his people and society at large. He must be focused on how to achieve his company's Goals and Objectives with Right Path and Right deeds. Only then his success will be everlasting and meaningful.

36

कबीरा ते नर अँध है, गुरु को कहते और।
हरि रूठे गुरु ठौर है, गुरु रूठे नहीं ठौर।।

Meaning

Kabir in this couplet says that those people are ignorant who does not understand the importance of Teacher or a learned person. So if God is angry with you, Teacher will come and show you the right path. But there is no one to show you right path, if your teacher is angry with you.

Lesson for Entrepreneurs

Through this Kabir Couplet we can derive the importance of the people who are learned and show the organisation the right direction. If anything is not going well in the organisation, then these people with knowledge and experience will show you the Right Path. But there is no person to show the right direction to the organisation, if these well wishers are annoyed and dissatisfied with the organisation or the working of the organisation. Hence, the entrepreneur should always look for advise by these people and follow their direction.

37

कबीर सुता क्या करे, जागी न जपे मुरारी।
एक दिन तू भी सोवेगा, लम्बे पाँव पसारी।।

Meaning

Kabir here wants to express that human beings are always sleeping or wasting their time in unnecessary things and do not remember God during their life. It is important to understand that we have to remember the God, otherwise the day will come that we will all be permanently sleeping or dead and will have no more time to remember God.

Lesson for Entrepreneurs

Thru this couplet of Kabir an entrepreneur should interpret that he is always running after materialistic things in his life and hardly doing any good work for others. One should earn profit in the business, but whatever is extra we should spend on other people or society. It is the true Profit of the Organisation. One should not be wasting their money on unnecessary things and focus on the welfare of the other person and society at large.

38

पोथी पढ़ पढ़ जग मुआ, पंडित भया न कोय।
ढाई आखर प्रेम का, पढ़े सो पंडित होय।।

Meaning

Kabir in this couplet try to tell that people who claim to be very knowledgeable and learned, after reading lots of books and religious scriptures, they forget loving the people around them. They forget that they are useless, if they do not love people around them. In Kabir opinion any person who knows how to love people and human beings at large, is more learned and knowledgeable than those who are just knowledgeable, by reading books and religious scripture.

Lesson for Entrepreneurs

Through this couplet of Kabir, we can derive the meaning that entrepreneur thinks to be successful if they earn profit and acquire materialistic wealth. But these successful entrepreneurs forget to make the people around them happy by making them part of this success. They forget the people who have helped them to achieve this success. In Kabir view the person is only successful if he shares his success with others and people of the organisation. He should only be successful, if he shares his materialistic wealth with the society at large, otherwise he is an unsuccessful entrepreneur, even if he has acquired great wealth for himself.

39

राम बुलावा भेजिया, दिया कबीरा रोय।
जो सुख साधू संग में, सो बैकुंठ न होय।।

Meaning

Kabir in this couplet express the Joy of Company of Learned People. He says that when the end comes to Him and God Rama send his angels to take the life of Kabir, Kabir starts crying. The reason was not because he was dying but the reason was that he will miss the company of learned people, which cannot be compensated by the all comforts of Heaven.

Lesson for Entrepreneurs

Through this couplet we can derive that an entrepreneur should always be happy to have more knowledgeable people in his organisation, rather than all the comfort he derives from the wealth, acquired by the business. According to Kabir no wealth and success can replace the joy of having good and learned people in his organisation, which can take the organisation to a new height.

40

शीलवंत सबसे बड़ा सब रतनन की खान।
तीन लोक की सम्पदा, रही शील में आन।।

Meaning

Here in this couplet Kabir try to say that the biggest and most expensive ornament is Calmness and Piousness. Those people who have these qualities are the richest and they have the wealth of all Three World. Hence, we should have real wealth rather than artificial wealth.

Lesson for Entrepreneurs

Through this couplet of Kabir, we can derive the meaning that an entrepreneur is always having greed for more and more wealth and artificial materialistic success. But the real wealth is to not be greedy but enjoy the wealth and success which is acquired by right and pious means. He should also share with people who are instrumental in bringing that wealth and success to the organisation. Those entrepreneurs do this are the real wealthy and successful entrepreneurs.

41

माखी गुड में गडी रहे, पंख रहे लिपटाए।
हाथ मले और सर धुनें, लालच बुरी बलाय।।

Meaning

Kabir here explains the concept of Greed. He says that when a Makkhi (FLY) sees Jaggery/Honey it gets attracted towards it. He sits on the it and cover it with all its face, wings and body. But after tasting it when it tries to fly it cannot, as he is now stick to Honey/jaggery. Then he starts repenting his Greed. Similarly, it is same for Human Being. Man is so busy in artificial Greed of materialistic things that when ends come he is sees that he has done nothing substantial for mankind or the society. He realises that he has just been running for money and success and profits and gave nothing back to society. He then starts repenting but it is of no use.

Lesson for Entrepreneurs

Thru this couplet of Kabir, we can realise that an entrepreneur is so involved in satisfying his Greed for materialistic things that forget to do good things in his life.

He is so obsessed with the accumulating wealth, getting profits for company, expansion of company etc. He forgets that he has done nothing in his life which is beneficial for the employees/ staff/stake holders and society at large. His contribution is nothing to society and mankind. He then starts repenting it in his last stages but that repenting is of no use as time has already gone.

42

कुटिल वचन सबसे बुरा, जा से होत न चार।
साधू वचन जल रूप है, बरसे अमृत धार।।

Meaning

Kabir here explains the importance of Good Words. In this couplet he says that anyone who speaks in bad tone or bad words, does no one's any good. Bad words do not solve any problems but in most of the cases it aggravates the problems. On the other hand, the Good Tone and Kind words of pure man, not only is good to listen but it also solves the problem by words only. Hence, we should be speaking only Kind words and Kind manner.

Lesson for Entrepreneurs

Through this couplet of Kabir's, we can derive the importance of Communication. It is very important for an entrepreneur to be a good communication person. How to speak, when to speak, how much to speak, what to speak etc is very important for the entrepreneur. Entrepreneur who knows how to do speak solves many problems and have growth and prosperity in business. On the other hand, even a successful entrepreneur who does not know how to speak destroys everything and become unsuccessful. Hence it is important to communicate well with your employees, your customer, your stakeholders etc to be a successful entrepreneur.

43

ऊँचे कुल का जनमिया, करनी ऊँची न होय।
सुवर्ण कलश सुरा भरा, साधू निंदा होय।।

Meaning

Here in this couplet Kabir says that it is immaterial if you are born in wealthy family and upper strata of society, if you have done nothing good for the society and people. It is worthless to have you born with money if you have not used it for good purpose. It is same like that you have a gold utensil but it is filled with Poison and is of No Use to anyone.

Lesson for Entrepreneurs

Through this couplet of Kabir's, we can derive the True meaning of Wealth. Kabir here wants to say that it is of no use to society that you are born in a wealthy family or you are a successful entrepreneur, unless you use this wealth for the society and mankind. Your wealth is good only if you use it for other people and your organisational people. It is important that you do Good Karma or Charitable work with your wealth, otherwise it is immaterial how much you earn and are wealthy or successful.

44

रात गंवाई सोय के, दिवस गंवाया खाय।
हीरा जन्म अमोल सा, कोड़ी बदले जाय।।

Meaning

Kabir through this couplet wants to say that a man spends his entire life in worthless things. In night he is sleeping and in daytime he works to earn. He forgets to remember for what he was born and got this life. He was born with a great purpose but he wasted that chance. He was precious when he was born but he became worthless when he dies. Hence understand the purpose of your life and do good deeds, while you are alive and serve the purpose of your birth in this world.

Lesson for Entrepreneurs

Through this couplet of Kabir, we can derive the True meaning of Wealth and Good deeds in life. According to Kabir, wealth and success has to be dealt differently by the entrepreneur, as it is for larger good for the society. Day and night entrepreneur is working to earn money and profits, but he fails to understand that this wealth and money is not for one person or one family. It is for all those who has helped him to be successful and that wealth is to be shared with those people and society at large. Wealth is given to entrepreneur for larger good deeds but he wastes it for his own needs and wishes, which is of no use and worthless.

45

कामी क्रोधी लालची, इनसे भक्ति न होय।
भक्ति करे कोई सुरमा, जाती बरन कुल खोए।।

Meaning

Kabir in this couplet says that a man who is Greedy, Immoral, filled with anger and hatred- cannot be close to God as he cannot impress God having all these shortcomings in character. Only that person is close to God who has left everything like his caste, religion, his family heritage, anger and arrogance. The person who is simple and kind is liked by God and has blessing of him.

Lesson for Entrepreneurs

Through this couplet of Kabir, we can derive that an entrepreneur cannot be respected and honoured by people, if he is filled with Greed, Treachery and Arrogance of his family heritage and wealth. He cannot be liked by any person who is not simple and kind in his heart. Hence to be loved by people the entrepreneur should always take care of the people who has contributed in his success and should not forget them. The entrepreneur should be always kind in heart and give back to society who has made him successful and wealthy.

46

कागा का को धन हरे, कोयल का को देय।
मीठे वचन सुना के, जग अपना कर लेय।।

Meaning

In this couplet Kabir says that although Crow does not take any money from anyone, but nobody likes crow because of his harsh voice. On the other hand, Koyal does not give any money to anyone, but everyone likes her because of her sweet voice. Hence good communication is important in life.

Lesson for Entrepreneurs

Through this Kabir couplet we can understand the importance of the communication. It is just not the tone of voice but what to say, how to say, when to say etc is also important. Lots of work can be done by an entrepreneur by the way he interacts with others and how he communicates with them. All successful people have this quality of good interpersonal skills and way to good communication. Lots of problems can be solved just by good communication and success can be achieved.

47

लूट सके तो लूट ले, हरी नाम की लूट।
अंत समय पछतायेगा, जब प्राण जायेगे छूट।।

Meaning

Kabir here says that human being is so ignorant that even God is present everywhere he forgets to remember him. He is so busy in other things that even he forgets to thank the God for whatever he achieves. Kabir says that it is still time to remember God and Thank him, because when end will come man can only repent and be sorrow that he did not remembered God.

Lesson for Entrepreneurs

From this couplet of Kabir, we can interpret that success and wealth comes with the Grace of God and we often forget God to thank him. There is always time in life that we remember God and do some good work in his name. But instead, we in pursuit of money, profit and success we forget God and Good Deeds. Hence when we have success and wealth, we should always do some good work in name of the God and thank him in our own way. Otherwise, everything is meaningless and at the end we will regret and feel sorry, that we could not do anything worth living.

48

तिनका कबहुँ ना निंदये, जो पाँव तले होय।
कबहुँ उड़ आँखो पड़े, पीर घनेरी होय।

Meaning

Kabir in this couplet says that small Tinka under your feet should not be ignored and humiliated. Because when this Tinka goes inside your eye it gives immense pain. Hence, we should always respect and give importance to smallest person in life and be grounded.

Lesson for Entrepreneurs

Through this couplet of Kabir we can derive the lesson that one should always give importance and value even to the smallest person in the organisation. It is often seen that went the organisation becomes big and successful, entrepreneur often forget the small employees and their contribution to the organisation. Entrepreneur stops giving the importance to these people. One should always remember that in organisation nobody is small or big, they are all contributing to the success of the organisation in their own way. Hence we should always give due respect and importance to all employees of the organisation, irrespective of their post and work.

49

धीरे-धीरे रे मना, धीरे सब कुछ होय।
माली सींचे सौ घड़ा, ऋतु आए फल होय।।

Meaning

Kabir in this couplet says that in this world everything will happen at its own pace. Things will not happen immediately as things take their own time. It is like that trees will not have flowers immediately if you pour more water, but it will happen only in the time of spring. Hence everyone should have patience and wait for the right time.

Lesson for Entrepreneurs

From this Kabir couplet we can derive the true meaning of patience. Here as an entrepreneur, we should not be in hurry to be successful and profitable. Success is a long journey and it takes its own time. There are no shortcuts for everlasting success and growth. If we adopt shortcuts or illegal means for making our business successful then it is permanent and bound to collapse. Hence, we should take a normal course of growth and successful journey which need patience and hard work. We cannot lose our patience to become a successful entrepreneur.

50

जो तोकूं कांटा बुवे, ताहि बोय तू फूल।
तोकू फूल के फूल हैं, बाकू हैं त्रिशूल।।

Meaning

It means that who sow horns for you, let them do that. But you must only sow flowers. Because if you do that you will get flowers only and other will get horns only. It implies that you should continue doing good work for others even others do bad work for you. You will always reap good results of your good deeds and other will get bad results of their bad deeds.

Lesson for Entrepreneurs

Kabir here says that when you are in business many competitors will adopt unfair means to push you out from the market. Never get afraid of these methods and keep doing your business in an ethical way. Competitors will automatically be out of business as unethical ways are very short term. Businesses which are ethically done will only continue in long run. Hence focus on your ethical business and forget about unfair business competitors. They will perish automatically sooner or later.